DUTCH OVEN

Breakfasts

DUTCH OVEN
Breakfasts

DEBBIE HAIR

PHOTOGRAPHS BY
SUSAN BARNSON HAYWARD

GIBBS SMITH
TO ENRICH AND INSPIRE HUMANKIND

First Edition
17 16 15 14 13   5 4 3 2 1

Text © 2013 Debbie Hair
Photographs © 2013 Susan Barnson Hayward

Published by
Gibbs Smith
P.O. Box 667
Layton, Utah 84041

1.800.835.4993 orders
www.gibbs-smith.com

Designed by Drew Furlong
Printed and bound in China
Gibbs Smith books are printed on either recycled, 100% post-consumer
waste, FSC-certified papers or on paper produced from sustainable PEFC-
certified forest/controlled wood source. Learn more at www.pefc.org.

Library of Congress Cataloging-in-Publication Data

Hair, Debbie.
  Dutch oven breakfasts / Debbie Hair ; photographs by Susan Barnson
Hayward. — First edition.
      pages cm
  Includes index.
  ISBN 978-1-4236-3228-3
1. Breakfasts. 2. Dutch oven cooking. I. Title.
  TX733.H346 2013
  641.5'2—dc23
                        2012050558

Eat breakfast like a king, lunch like a prince, and dinner like a pauper.

Adelle Davis

This book is dedicated to:

Dick and Pam Stucki, for teaching me Dutch oven magic; Cindy Ayres, for teaching me how to play with my food; and my mom, Sharon Duncan, who always let me explore my love of cooking.

A note of thanks to my family and the Dutch oven folks who have been a constant source of encouragement for my Dutch oven endeavors.

CONTENTS

INTRODUCTION 8

EGGS 16

POTATOES 34

PANCAKES, FRENCH
TOAST, AND CREPES 48

BREADS AND PASTRIES 64

BREAKFAST CASSEROLES 96

FAMILY FAVORITES 114

INDEX 123

INTRODUCTION

Magic! I love magic and trying to figure out the sleight of hand. Dutch ovens are magical. I remember as a young girl watching Dutch oven cooks work magic and then placing the best food on our plates. When I moved to Utah, some of my new neighbors were legendary Dutch oven cooks. They allowed me to tag along on a few of their catering gigs to "help" them cook. From these experiences, I was able to learn the sleight of hand. That is, the technique of producing fabulous food from the cast iron vessel. The trick is using a good recipe, quality ingredients, and understanding proper heat control. I hope this book helps you enjoy the magic!

DUTCH OVEN HEAT CONTROL

Dutch ovens are well known for their baking capability, but they also can be used for simmering, boiling, sautéing, broiling, deep frying, and even freezing ice cream.

The number one rule of Dutch oven cooking is that it is easier to add heat to a Dutch oven than it is to cool a hot oven down. Start with a conservative number of coals and then add more if necessary.

When baking, the heat source comes from both underneath and on top of the Dutch oven. See the below chart for a handy guide to know how many coals to place underneath the oven and how many coals to place on top of the oven to achieve a specific baking temperature. Place the bottom coals in a ring about the size of the oven. Set the oven over the ring and then place the top coals on the lid along the flange in a ring toward the outer edge.

BAKING TEMPERATURE CHART

OVEN	325°	350°	375°	400°	425°	450°
8-INCH	5/10	5/11	5/12	6/12	6/13	6/14
10-INCH	6/13	7/14	7/16	8/17	9/18	10/19
12-INCH	7/16	8/17	9/18	10/19	10/21	11/22
14-INCH	10/20	11/21	12/22	12/24	13/25	14/26

The coal ratio is bottom coals/top coals

When simmering and sautéing, the heat source comes from underneath the Dutch oven. Use the diameter of the oven to determine the number of coals that should be placed under it. The general rule is the diameter times 2. For example,

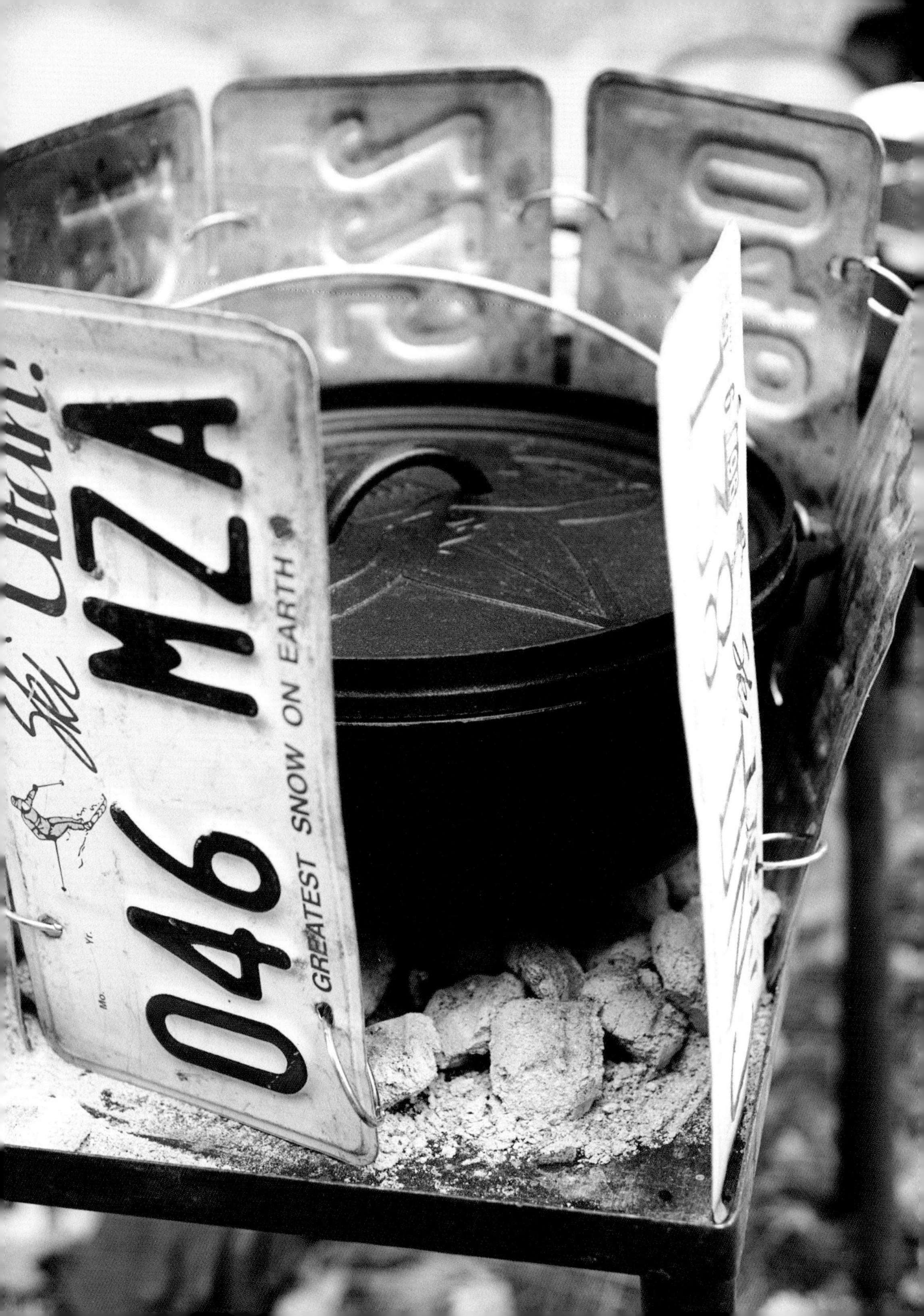
Ski Utah!
046 MZA
GREATEST SNOW ON EARTH

a 12-inch Dutch oven would need 24 coals. If you need a slower simmer or sauté, reduce the number of coals by 4.

When deep frying, the heat source comes from underneath the Dutch oven. A full bed of coals is necessary. Use a thermometer and adjust the number of coals to achieve 375–400 degrees. Begin with number of coals equaling the diameter of the Dutch oven doubled and add from there.

When broiling, all the heat is on the lid. Use the number of coals equaling the diameter of the Dutch oven doubled.

The above information is a good starting point; however, you often need to make heat adjustments due to weather conditions. If cooking when the weather is cooler than 60 degrees, you will need to add a few more coals—1 underneath the oven and 2 on the lid (more if using a large oven). If cooking in 90 degree weather or above, consider reducing the number of coals.

If cooking in high altitudes, add more heat. Cooking times will also take longer.

No matter what the conditions, always keep your eye on your pots and adjust as necessary. And as Dutch oven expert Colleen Sloan teaches, "You will not need a timer to tell when your dishes are done. Your nose will tell ya!"

USEFUL TOOLS

Gloves with long sleeves for protecting hands and arms from the heat.

Lid lifters for lifting very hot lids.

Long handled tongs for moving hot coals.

Trivets to set the lid on so that it is not on the ground. Trivets can be used to keep hot ovens off tables and will also hold your lid upside down so it can be used as a griddle.

A whisk broom to brush the ashes off the lids of the Dutch ovens.

A cook table is great. It lifts your work area off the ground and prevents you from bending over so much.

A metal bucket to hold the spent coals.

A windbreak of some type to help keep your coals burning evenly on a windy day. I use old license plates and stand them on end. The windbreaks provided with cook tables are often too short to protect the coals on the lid of the Dutch oven. A binder ring can be used to connect the plates together.

HELPFUL HINTS

LIGHTING COALS

The standard method for lighting coals is to stack the number of needed coals in a pyramid. Soak with lighter fluid and then light with a match and let them burn until the corners of the coals become white.

But my favorite way to light the coals is a bit easier—use a charcoal chimney (or sometimes called a basket) and a propane stove. Place the number of coals needed in the chimney and set on the stove. Light the stove and turn the flame up high. Let the coals burn for about 5 minutes and then shake the chimney so that the top coals shake down to the bottom. Put the chimney back on the flame for a few more minutes. When the corners of the coals are white, they are hot and ready.

SEASONING YOUR DUTCH OVEN

Most Dutch ovens come preseasoned, but I prefer to clean and oil any new oven. This is also how you prepare a new Dutch oven that has not been preseasoned. Wash, rinse, and dry your Dutch oven and lid. Rub a layer of oil on the inside and outside of your oven and lid and bake in a 450 degree oven for 30 minutes. The oil may smoke as it is burned into the pores of the Dutch oven. After the oven has cooled, wipe off any excess oil and store with paper towels placed inside your oven. Allow the edge of the paper towels to partly hang outside the oven. This will allow for air circulation and will prevent rust from forming.

CLEANING YOUR DUTCH OVEN

Cleaning a Dutch oven is fairly easy. Scrape out any leftover food with a stiff plastic brush or plastic scraper and rinse oven with warm water to completely remove any food particles. Dry oven over heat (over open flame, coals, or in your kitchen oven) just long enough to completely dry your oven. Wipe with an oiled cloth to coat oven with thin layer of oil. This will protect the seasoning and prevent rusting. Do not be tempted to use too much oil. If you use too much oil or store for a long period of time, the oil may turn rancid.

STORING YOUR DUTCH OVEN

After you clean your Dutch oven, place a couple of paper towels in the bottom and up the sides of the oven and allow an edge to hang out under the lid so that air can circulate. Store ovens in a cool dry place.

BISCUIT TIPS

It is easy to overwork biscuit dough. Overworked dough will cause the biscuits to turn out tough.

Use a fork to cut in shortening into the dry ingredients.

When adding liquids, use a fork and work quickly.

Knead dough only a few times and roll dough only as many times as it takes to get desired thickness.

Biscuits will rise better if the dough is cut without using a twisting motion, and cut biscuits as close together as possible. Be gentle when pressing the dough scraps together for a second cutting. The second biscuits will not rise as nicely as the first cut ones.

If you like crusty biscuits, place them apart from one another to bake. If you prefer the soft edges then place the biscuits close together so they are barley touching.

BREAD TIPS

Baking bread is very satisfying, but it can be really disappointing. Here are a few tricks to ensure success.

Proof the yeast. This can be done by dissolving the yeast in a small amount of warm water. The temperature of the water should be 105–115 degrees. Allow this to set for about 5 minutes. The yeast should produce a nice foamy head on the water.

Sugar will speed yeast growth and salt retards the growth.

Knead the bread for about 10 minutes. This will work the gluten in the bread. Gluten is the elastic quality in wheat flour. It will stretch with the gas produced by the yeast and trap the bubbles to give the bread volume.

The air temperature will determine how fast your bread will rise. The optimum temperature is 85 degrees.

To see if the bread is done, inset an instant read thermometer. When the bread reaches 180–200 degrees, it is done.

The recipes in this book can be cooked indoors using your home oven or stovetop. Simply follow the directions to include cooking temperatures and times.

EGGS

THE BASIC OMELET 17

DENVER OMELET 19

ITALIAN SAUSAGE OMELET 20

TAPAS, A SPANISH OMELET 22

SPANISH SCRAMBLED EGGS 23

PICTURE PERFECT EGGS AND TOAST 25

CLASSIC QUICHE LORRAINE 26

BLUE CHEESE QUICHE 28

EASY CRUST-LESS QUICHE 30

EGGS BENEDICT 31

THE BASIC OMELET

Serves 2

10-INCH DUTCH OVEN
8 COALS ON BOTTOM
12 COALS ON TOP
350 DEGREES

4 eggs, separated
2 tablespoons water
¼ teaspoon salt
1 tablespoon butter
½ cup grated sharp cheddar cheese

In a medium bowl, beat egg whites until foamy; add water and salt. Continue beating until stiff peaks form. Beat egg yolks in a medium bowl until thick and lemon colored. Fold whites into yolks.

Place Dutch oven over 8 coals. When the oven is hot, add butter and coat the bottom of the oven. Spread egg mixture in oven. Cover and bake, using 8 coals underneath the oven and 12 coals on top, for 10 minutes or until a knife inserted in the center comes out clean. Sprinkle cheese on top of omelet. Use a flexible spatula to loosen omelet and fold. Cut omelet in half to serve.

NOTE: *This recipe is easily doubled for 4 servings. Bake in a 12-inch Dutch oven, using 8 coals underneath the oven and 16 coals on top.*

VARIATION: Any of the following ingredients may be added to the basic omelet; sliced mushrooms, chopped onion, chopped bell pepper, minced cooked ham, crumbled cooked sausage or bacon, and herbs of choice.

This is a gluten-free recipe.

DENVER OMELET

Serves 2

10-INCH DUTCH OVEN
8 COALS ON BOTTOM
12 COALS ON TOP
350 DEGREES

2 tablespoons butter
¼ cup chopped onion
½ cup chopped red bell pepper
½ cup chopped green bell pepper
½ cup diced cooked ham
8 slices bacon, cooked
   and crumbled

4 eggs
½ teaspoon salt
½ teaspoon pepper
½ cup grated cheddar
   cheese, optional

Place Dutch oven over 8 coals and use oven like a skillet. Melt butter and stir in onion and bell peppers. Sauté until onion is translucent. Add the ham and bacon.

In a small bowl, beat the eggs. Add salt and pepper. Gently stir eggs into mixture in bottom of Dutch oven. Cover and bake, using 8 coals underneath the oven and 12 coals on top, for about 3 minutes, until the bottom of the eggs are lightly browned. Use a flexible spatula to loosen omelet and turn. Replace the lid and bake until underside is browned, about 5 minutes. Sprinkle cheese over omelet, if using. Fold omelet and cut in half to serve.

VARIATION: To make omelet fluffier, separate the egg whites and whip until stiff peaks form. Fold beaten egg yolks into the egg whites. Pour over vegetables and gently stir.

🍃 This is a gluten-free recipe.

ITALIAN SAUSAGE OMELET

Serves 6

12-INCH DUTCH OVEN
12 COALS ON BOTTOM
12 COALS ON TOP
350 DEGREES

½ pound ground hot Italian sausage
½ cup chopped green bell pepper
½ cup chopped yellow onion
6 eggs, beaten

Place Dutch oven over 12 coals and use oven like a skillet. Brown sausage and then add bell pepper and onion and cook until bell pepper is tender and onion translucent, about 3 minutes. Pour in eggs. Stir just a little as if cooking scrambled eggs; this will help the uncooked egg reach the bottom of the oven. Do not over stir. Cover and bake, using 12 coals underneath the oven and 12 coals on top, for 10 minutes or until eggs are set. Use a spatula to cut the omelet into 6 servings.

🌿 This is a gluten-free recipe.

TAPAS, A SPANISH OMELET

Serves 4

12-INCH DUTCH OVEN
10 COALS ON BOTTOM
14 COALS ON TOP
350 DEGREES

½ cup olive oil
2 cups thinly sliced potatoes
½ cup chopped onion
1 teaspoon seasoned salt

4 eggs
Salt, optional
Salsa

Place Dutch oven over all 24 coals and use oven like a skillet. Heat the oil and then add the potatoes, onion, and seasoned salt. Fry potatoes, stirring only occasionally, until golden brown. Remove Dutch oven from the heat and drain off oil as much as possible.

In a small bowl, beat the eggs well and add salt, if using; mix with the potatoes.

Cover and bake, using 10 coals underneath the oven and 14 coals on top, until the omelet seems nearly cooked, about 6 minutes. Shake oven to loosen omelet from the bottom. Use a flexible spatula to turn omelet over to finish cooking. Using heavy gloves, invert the oven, set it down on a trivet, and remove the oven off the lid. Serve the omelet from the lid with salsa.

VARIATION: Add sliced mushrooms, olives, and bell pepper.

This is a gluten-free recipe.

SPANISH SCRAMBLED EGGS

Serves 6

12-INCH DUTCH OVEN
24 COALS ON BOTTOM

¼ cup chopped green bell pepper
¼ cup finely chopped scallions
6 eggs
¼ cup milk
⅛ teaspoon pepper
⅛ teaspoon hot sauce

½ cup chopped tomato
¼ cup grated sharp
  cheddar cheese
Pimiento and fresh parsley
  springs, for garnish

Place Dutch oven over all 24 coals and use oven like a skillet. Prepare oven with nonstick cooking spray. Sauté the bell pepper and scallions until tender, about 3 minutes. Remove from oven and set aside.

In a large bowl, combine eggs, milk, pepper, and hot sauce; beat well. Pour into oven. Cook over heat, gently stirring until eggs are set. Stir in cooked vegetables and tomato; cook until heated. Sprinkle with cheese. Garnish with pimiento and parsley.

❧ This is a gluten-free recipe.

PICTURE PERFECT EGGS AND TOAST

Serves 8

14-INCH DUTCH OVEN
28 COALS ON BOTTOM

4 tablespoons canola oil or butter, divided,
   plus additional for brushing
8 slices bread
8 eggs
Pepper, to taste
Grated Parmesan cheese

Place Dutch oven over all 28 coals and use oven like a skillet.

Brush oil on each side of the bread slices. Use a 3-inch biscuit cutter to cut a circle in the center of each slice of bread. Reserve the cutout circles. Heat 2 tablespoons oil in bottom of oven. Place cutout circles in the oven and cook for a few minutes until toasted. Remove to a holding plate and cover with aluminum foil to keep warm.

Place 4 bread slices in oven and cook until bottoms are toasted, about 1–2 minutes. Flip and then crack an egg into each hole. Season the toast and egg with pepper and cheese. Cook to desired doneness, 2–3 minutes for soft yolks. Remove from oven to holding plate and cover with foil to keep warm. Repeat with remaining ingredients. Garnish with reserved cutouts.

CLASSIC QUICHE LORRAINE

Serves 6–8

12-INCH DUTCH OVEN
8 COALS ON BOTTOM
16 COALS ON TOP
350 DEGREES

½ pound bacon, chopped
    in ½-inch pieces
1 cup chopped onion
½ cup diced mushrooms
1 (10-inch) pie crust in
    pie pan, unbaked
3 cups grated white
    cheddar cheese

2 eggs, slightly beaten
1 cup milk
½ teaspoon salt
⅛ teaspoon pepper
¼ teaspoon nutmeg
¼ cup bread crumbs

Place Dutch oven over all 24 coals and use oven like a skillet. Fry the bacon and pour off about half of the fat. Add onion and mushrooms and cook until onion is translucent. Remove bacon, onion, and mushrooms from Dutch oven and put into the pie crust. Sprinkle with cheese. Wipe out the Dutch oven so that it is clean.

In a small bowl, combine eggs, milk, salt, pepper, and nutmeg and pour over cheese and vegetables. Scatter bread crumbs evenly over the top.

Place 3 canning jar rings in bottom of Dutch oven and set pie pan on the rings. (This will allow air to circulate under the pie pan.) Cover and bake, using 8 coals underneath the oven and 16 coals on top, for 30–35 minutes. Quiche should be lightly browned. Let set to cool before serving.

VARIATION: The pie crust can be pressed into the bottom of the Dutch oven and quiche baked directly in the oven. To do this, use a 10-inch oven, using 7 coals underneath the oven and 13 on top. Bake for 30 minutes. If you would like to lift the quiche out of the oven for serving, use parchment paper lifts—2 long strips of paper placed across the bottom of the oven before the pie crust is added. When quiche is baked and cooled you can lift the quiche from the Dutch oven.

BLUE CHEESE QUICHE

Serves 6–8

2 (10-INCH) DUTCH OVENS
7 COALS ON BOTTOM
13 COALS ON TOP
350 DEGREES

⅔ cup fine bread crumbs

3 tablespoons melted
butter, divided

½ cup chopped onion

2 packages (8 ounces each) cream
cheese cut into 1-inch cubes

½ cup crumbled blue cheese

⅓ cup sour cream

2 tablespoons fresh parsley

4 eggs

⅛ teaspoon salt

⅛ teaspoon white pepper

Fresh parsley sprigs

Grease bottom and sides of 1 Dutch oven. In a small bowl, combine bread crumbs with 2 tablespoons butter. Press bread crumbs into the bottom of the oven and 1 inch up the sides.

Place second Dutch oven over all 20 coals and use oven like a skillet. Sauté onion in remaining butter until translucent. In a large bowl, whisk together onion, cream cheese, blue cheese, sour cream, and parsley. Add eggs and seasonings; whisk until eggs are foamy, about 2 minutes.

Pour into Dutch oven prepared with bread crumbs. Cover and bake, using 7 coals underneath the oven and 13 coals on top, for 30–40 minutes. Garnish with parsley.

VARIATION: If you want this recipe to be gluten free, use dried gluten-free bread to make bread crumbs.

EASY CRUST—LESS QUICHE

Serves 6–8

10-INCH DUTCH OVEN
7 COALS ON BOTTOM
13 COALS ON TOP
350 DEGREES

2½ cups small curd
   cottage cheese

½ cup grated mozzarella cheese

1 green onion, chopped

½ cup chopped fresh parsley

1 egg

3 egg whites, whipped
   to stiff peaks

1 teaspoon dry mustard

1½ tablespoons grated
   Parmesan cheese

Prepare Dutch oven with nonstick cooking spray. In a large bowl, combine cottage cheese, mozzarella cheese, onion, parsley, egg, egg whites, and mustard. Spread mixture into bottom of Dutch oven. Sprinkle Parmesan cheese on the top. Cover and bake, using 7 coals underneath the oven and 13 coals on top, for 30 minutes.

❧ This is a gluten-free recipe.

EGGS BENEDICT

Serves 8

2 (12-INCH) DUTCH OVENS
36 COALS ON BOTTOM

8 eggs
Water
2 teaspoons white vinegar
8 slices Canadian bacon
4 English muffins
Butter
Parsley sprigs

HOLLANDAISE SAUCE

1 cup butter
6 egg yolks
2 tablespoons lemon juice
½ teaspoon salt
Dash cayenne or Tabasco sauce

Place 1 Dutch oven over 24 coals and set 4 ramekins in Dutch oven. Add water until level reaches halfway up the ramekins. Add vinegar to water and bring to a boil. Use this water bath to poach eggs. Process the eggs one at a time. Crack an egg into a ramekin and wait until it starts to cook before adding the second egg into the second ramekin. Work clockwise to keep track of cooking eggs. (Eggs can be cooked directly in the water.) When cooked to desired doneness, remove to a warmed plate. Eggs will take the longest to cook.

Keep your eye on the eggs, and while waiting for them to cook, prepare muffins and bacon. Place second Dutch oven over 12 coals. Melt 1 cup butter in bottom of oven and then pour into a small bowl to reserve for Hollandaise Sauce. Fry bacon in oven, turning once as it browns. When browned on both sides, remove and wrap in aluminum foil to keep warm. Toast English muffins on bottom of oven. When toasted, remove and wrap in foil to keep warm.

HOLLANDAISE SAUCE

Place egg yolks, lemon juice, and salt in a blender and blend on medium for 30 seconds. Eggs should be light in color. Set blender on slowest speed and

continued

gradually add in reserved butter while continuing to blend. Pour into a container that can be kept warm so the butter will not set up.

To serve; butter the toasted muffin halves, cover with a slice of bacon, place a poached egg on top of the bacon, and pour Hollandaise sauce over the muffin. Garnish with parsley.

NOTE: *To make while camping, use biscuit cutters on the bottom of the oven to contain eggs in a circular shape and fry eggs instead of poaching. Simmering takes forever in high altitudes. A protein shaker will adequately blend the Hollandaise Sauce.*

POTATOES

COWBOY CREAMIES 35

BREAKFAST BURRITOS 36

GERMAN POTATO PANCAKES 38

SUNRISE POTATOES 39

POTATO SPEARS 40

DUTCH OVEN SPARKLING POTATOES 43

FIREHOUSE HASH 44

BREAKFAST HASH 45

SCOTCH EGGS 46

COWBOY CREAMIES

Serves 8

12-INCH DUTCH OVEN
9 COALS ON BOTTOM
15 COALS ON TOP
350 DEGREES

½ pound bacon

1 medium yellow onion, thinly sliced

3 pounds small red potatoes, thinly sliced

2 cups heavy cream

¼ teaspoon thyme

1½ teaspoons minced garlic

1¼ teaspoons salt

½ teaspoon pepper

1 cup grated cheddar cheese

Paprika

Place Dutch oven over 12 coals and use oven like a skillet. Brown the bacon in the bottom of the Dutch oven. Pour off fat and crumble bacon. Add onion and potatoes and stir into bacon.

In a small bowl, mix cream, thyme, garlic, salt, and pepper; pour over potato mixture. Cover and bake, using 9 coals underneath the oven and 15 coals on top, for about an hour. When potatoes are tender, remove oven from heat and stir in cheese, saving some cheese to sprinkle on top. Put potatoes back on heat for about 10 more minutes or until cheese melts. Sprinkle paprika on top just before serving.

ᗭ This is a gluten-free recipe.

BREAKFAST BURRITOS

Serves 6

12-INCH DUTCH OVEN
24 COALS ON BOTTOM

⅓ pound ground country-
style sausage

2 tablespoons vegetable oil

¼ cup chopped onion

½ pound potatoes, cooked
until just tender, diced

1 tablespoon chopped green chile

4 eggs, beaten

Salt and pepper, to taste

½ cup grated cheddar cheese

6 (8-inch) flour tortillas

Place Dutch oven over all 24 coals and use oven like a skillet. Brown the sausage and drain off fat; set aside in a medium bowl.

Heat the oil in oven and sauté onion until translucent. Add potatoes and chiles and cook for 2 minutes, stirring occasionally. Add eggs and stir mixture, scraping sides and bottom of oven until eggs are set, 3–5 minutes. Salt and pepper generously. Sprinkle cheese on top and cover with the lid for a few minutes to melt the cheese.

Divide mixture between tortillas, tuck ends, and roll up. This can be served immediately or wrapped in foil to keep warm.

NOTE: *Warming the tortillas before filling them will help prevent cracks.*

GERMAN POTATO PANCAKES

Serves 6–8

12-INCH DUTCH OVEN
20 COALS ON BOTTOM

6 large potatoes, peeled
  and shredded
1 onion, shredded
2 eggs
½ cup flour

1 teaspoon salt
1 tablespoon pepper
I tablespoon olive oil
Applesauce

In a large bowl, combine potatoes, onion, eggs, flour, salt, and pepper; mix well.

Place Dutch oven over all 20 coals and use oven like a skillet. Heat the oil in bottom of oven. Drop the potato mixture by spoonfuls into the oven and flatten pancakes to approximately ¼ inch thick. Fry the pancakes for about 1 minute, until golden brown. Flip the pancakes and brown other sides Serve hot and topped with applesauce.

SUNRISE POTATOES

Serves 8

12-INCH DUTCH OVEN
24 COALS ON BOTTOM

¼ cup butter

8 medium baked potatoes,
  diced or sliced*

1 yellow onion, chopped

1 red bell pepper, chopped

1 green bell pepper, chopped

½ tablespoon paprika

Salt and pepper, to taste

Place the Dutch oven over all 24 coals and use the oven like a skillet. Melt butter in the bottom of the oven. Add potatoes, onion, and bell peppers; fry, bringing the potatoes from the bottom of the oven with a spatula for even cooking and browning. Season with paprika, salt, and pepper just prior to serving.

*If you are camping, bake the potatoes the night before while your campfire is winding down. Wrap potatoes in foil and bake them in the coals of the fire. Be sure to rotate the potatoes so they cook evenly.

VARIATION: Add a ½ pound of bacon. Fry bacon and crumble then use the bacon grease instead of butter.

❧ This is a gluten-free recipe.

POTATO SPEARS

Serves 8

12-INCH DUTCH OVEN
9 COALS ON BOTTOM
15 COALS ON TOP
350 DEGREES

2 large long potatoes

8 slices bacon

¼ cup butter, softened

¼ cup honey

¼ teaspoon pepper

2 tablespoons minced onion

1 teaspoon chopped fresh
  parsley leaves

Cut potatoes into fourths lengthwise. Wrap each piece of potato with a strip of bacon and secure with toothpick. Place potato spears into Dutch oven, cover, and bake, using 9 coals underneath the oven and 15 coals on top, for 30–40 minutes. Turn occasionally with tongs.

Meanwhile, in a medium bowl, mix the butter, honey, pepper, onion, and parsley until thoroughly combined to create a glaze. When potatoes are baked, toss in the glaze and serve immediately.

❧ This is a gluten-free recipe.

DUTCH OVEN SPARKLING POTATOES

Serves 8

12-INCH DUTCH OVEN
9 COALS ON BOTTOM
15 COALS ON TOP
350 DEGREES

1 pound bacon, diced
2 yellow onions, sliced
8 medium potatoes, cubed
1 teaspoon seasoned salt
12 ounces Sprite
½ cup grated cheddar cheese

Place Dutch oven over all 24 coals and use oven like a skillet. Cook the bacon and onions until golden. Leave the onion mixture at the bottom of oven and layer the potatoes on top. Add seasoned salt and Sprite.

Cover and bake, using 9 coals underneath the oven and 15 coals on top, for 30–45 minutes until potatoes are tender. Add cheese and melt.

VARIATION: You can add chopped red or green bell pepper or mushrooms along with the potatoes.

❧ This is a gluten-free recipe.

FIREHOUSE HASH

Serves 4

12-INCH DUTCH OVEN
24 COALS ON BOTTOM

2 quarts water
4 large potatoes, diced
2 tablespoons olive oil
1 onion, diced small
1 green bell pepper, diced small
2 cloves garlic, minced

1 jalapeño pepper, diced small
Cayenne pepper, to taste
1 cup sour cream, optional
½ cup grated cheddar
  cheese, optional

Place Dutch oven over all 24 coals. Bring water to a boil. Add potatoes and cook about 15 minutes until just tender. Drain potatoes and set aside.

Dry oven and return to coals. Using the oven as a skillet, heat the oil and sauté the onion, bell pepper, and garlic. Add in the potatoes and stir occasionally until browned. Stir the jalapeño pepper and cayenne into the potatoes and remove oven from heat. Let potatoes sit for about 3 minutes before serving. Serve with a dollop of sour cream and a sprinkle of cheese, if using.

꒰ This is a gluten-free recipe.

BREAKFAST HASH

Serves 8

12-INCH DUTCH OVEN
8 COALS ON BOTTOM
17 COALS ON TOP
350 DEGREES

4 eggs, lightly beaten
½ cup grated Parmesan cheese
1 cup milk
½ cup sour cream
6 tablespoons butter, diced
1 yellow onion, chopped

1 tablespoon lemon juice
1 teaspoon pepper
1 teaspoon onion powder
1 teaspoon garlic powder
1 (30-ounce) bag frozen
  O'Brien potatoes

In a large bowl, mix eggs, cheese, milk, sour cream, butter, onion, lemon juice, pepper, onion powder, and garlic powder together. Fold in potatoes.

Oil Dutch oven and add potato mixture. Cover and bake, using 8 coals underneath the oven and 17 coals on top, for about an hour or until potatoes are browned.

This is a gluten-free recipe.

SCOTCH EGGS

Serves 8

12-INCH DUTCH OVEN
8 COALS ON BOTTOM
17 COALS ON TOP
350 DEGREES

2 pounds ground sausage
8 hard-boiled eggs
1 (30-ounce) bag frozen hash brown potatoes
1 recipe Country Gravy (page 71)

Flatten ¼ pound sausage and mold it around an egg until the egg is completely covered. Do this for each egg.

Place Dutch oven over all 25 coals and use oven like a skillet. Put the sausage-wrapped eggs in the Dutch oven and cook until browned, rolling so that all sides are evenly cooked. This will take about 15 minutes. Add in hash browns. Cover and bake, using 8 coals underneath the oven and 17 coals on top, for 30 minutes. Serve with a generous helping of gravy.

NOTE: *This recipe is gluten free if you don't serve it with the gravy.*

VARIATION: You can coat the sausage-covered eggs with bread crumbs and deep fry them.

PANCAKES, FRENCH TOAST, AND CREPES

MY FAVORITE PANCAKES 49

HOOTENANNY PANCAKE 50

STUFFED PANCAKES 53

FLUFFY APPLE PANCAKE 55

FRENCH TOAST SOUFFLÉ 56

FRENCH TOAST DUMPLINGS 58

AEBLESKIVERS 59

STRAWBERRY AND CREAM CREPES 61

CHOCOLATE CREPES 62

MY FAVORITE PANCAKES

Makes 8 (4-inch) pancakes

12-INCH DUTCH OVEN LID
24 COALS ON BOTTOM

1¼ cups flour
3 teaspoons baking powder
1 tablespoon sugar
½ teaspoon salt

1 egg, beaten
1 cup milk
2 tablespoons canola oil

Use a trivet to hold the lid of the Dutch oven upside down and level so that the lid becomes a griddle. Place the Dutch oven lid over all 24 coals.

In a large bowl, sift together flour, baking powder, sugar, and salt. In a small bowl, combine egg, milk, and oil; stir into dry ingredients until just moistened. When lid is hot, brush with a bit of oil and slowly pour pancake batter onto the lid. A 12-inch lid will cook 3–4 pancakes at a time. Pancake batter will bubble. When most of the bubbles have disappeared, turn the pancakes over to cook other side. When both sides are browned, remove from lid and serve.

NOTE: *If the pancake batter is a little on the thick side, the slope in the Dutch oven lid will not present a problem. Some of the larger Dutch oven lids do not have a slope.*

VARIATIONS: For blueberry pancakes, when the first sides of the pancakes are nicely browned, sprinkle some blueberries over each pancake. Turn pancake to brown other side. Try sliced strawberries, peaches, apples, or any fresh fruit, or chocolate chips or butterscotch chips. Whipped cream over the top is always a hit!

HOOTENANNY PANCAKE

Serves 8–10

12-INCH DUTCH OVEN
8 COALS ON BOTTOM
20 COALS ON TOP
375 DEGREES

½ cup butter
6 eggs
1 cup milk
½ cup sugar
1 teaspoon salt
1 cup flour

Place Dutch oven over 8 coals and melt butter in bottom of oven. Vigorously whisk together the eggs, milk, sugar, and salt then gradually add the flour. Pour into Dutch oven over melted butter. Cover and bake, using 8 coals underneath the oven and 20 coals on top, for about 25 minutes or until pancake is brown and fluffy. Cut into wedges and serve with butter, syrup, or jam.

NOTE: *Rice flour may be substituted for flour so that the pancake is gluten free. The pancake is a little denser but turns out satisfactory.*

HOMEMADE SYRUP

3 cups sugar, divided
2 cups warm water, divided
1 teaspoon vanilla or maple flavoring
A pinch of salt

continued

Place 1 cup sugar in a heavy-bottom saucepan. Add ½ cup water and stir constantly over medium heat. Stir until sugar boils. It will start turning a nice amber color. Keep sugar moving until desired color is reached. Slowly stir in remaining warm water and then remaining sugar. Stirring constantly, bring liquid back to a boil. Remove from heat when desired thickness is reached. Add flavoring. Serve warm.

NOTE: *Do not cook too long—if syrup reaches temperatures higher than 250 degrees, you will end up with candy.*

STUFFED PANCAKES

Makes 8 (4-inch) pancakes

12-INCH DUTCH OVEN LID
24 COALS ON BOTTOM

1 1/4 cups flour
3 teaspoons baking powder
1 tablespoon sugar
1/2 teaspoon salt
1 egg, beaten

1 cup milk
2 tablespoons canola oil
1 cup chocolate-hazelnut
  spread or Fruit Filling*

Use a trivet to hold the lid of the Dutch oven upside down and level so that the lid becomes a griddle. Place the Dutch oven lid over all 24 coals.

In a large bowl, sift together flour, baking powder, sugar, and salt. In a small bowl, combine egg, milk, and oil; stir into dry ingredients until just moistened. When lid is hot, brush with a bit of oil and slowly pour 1/4 cup batter onto the lid. Add a teaspoon chocolate-hazelnut spread or fruit filling to the center of the pancake and cover with a little more batter. A 12-inch lid will cook 3–4 pancakes at a time. Cook until the edges of the pancakes are dry and until most of the bubbles have disappeared; turn pancake over to cook other side. When both sides are browned, remove from lid and serve.

*FRUIT FILLING

1 package (8 ounces) cream
  cheese, softened
1/3 cup whipped cream
1/2 teaspoon vanilla

1/2 cup powdered sugar
1 cup blueberries,
  raspberries, blackberries,
  or sliced strawberries

In a large bowl, mix the first 4 ingredients together then gently stir in fruit.

VARIATION: Rather than making small pancakes, bake large a pancake then spread filling on pancake and fold in half.

FLUFFY APPLE PANCAKE

Serves 4–6

10-INCH DUTCH OVEN
7 COALS ON BOTTOM
16 COALS ON TOP
375 DEGREES

¾ cup pancake mix
½ cup milk
3 eggs
½ cup sugar, divided
¼ cup butter

4 cups peeled and thinly
   sliced tart apples
¼ cup pecan halves, chopped
1 teaspoon cinnamon

Place Dutch oven over 19 coals to preheat.

In a medium bowl, stir together pancake mix, milk, eggs, and 1 teaspoon sugar. Set aside.

In bottom of Dutch oven, melt butter and then sauté apples until tender. Sprinkle pecans, remaining sugar, and cinnamon over the apples. Carefully pour batter over apple mixture. Cover and bake, using 7 coals underneath the oven and 16 coals on top, for about 10 minutes or until pancake is fluffy. Using heavy gloves, invert the oven, set on a trivet, and remove the oven off the lid. Cut into wedges and serve.

FRENCH TOAST SOUFFLÉ

Serves 8–10

12-INCH DUTCH OVEN
9 COALS ON BOTTOM
18 COALS ON TOP
350 DEGREES

½ cup sugar

2 tablespoons cinnamon

8 to 10 slices bread,
  crusts removed

8 ounces cream cheese

12 eggs, beaten

⅓ cup maple syrup

2 cups milk

1 teaspoon vanilla

In a small bowl, combine sugar and cinnamon; set aside. Cut bread into cubes and place half in bottom of Dutch oven. Cut cream cheese into cubes and place on top of bread. Sprinkle with some of the cinnamon sugar. Top with remaining bread and sprinkle with cinnamon sugar.

In a large bowl, combine eggs, syrup, milk, and vanilla. Pour over bread and cheese. Cover and refrigerate overnight.

In the morning, bake, using 9 coals underneath the oven and 18 coals on top, for about 45 minutes or until firm and lightly browned.

NOTE: *This recipe can be successfully made with gluten-free bread.*

FRENCH TOAST DUMPLINGS

Serves 4–6

12-INCH DUTCH OVEN
24 COALS ON BOTTOM

1½ cups maple syrup
⅓ cup brown sugar
1 can refrigerator croissant rolls
1 teaspoon nutmeg
1 cup cinnamon sugar (1 part
    cinnamon 2 parts sugar)

Place Dutch oven over all 24 coals and use oven like a skillet. Add syrup and brown sugar and bring to a simmer. Cut each croissant into quarters and roll into a ball. Carefully drop each ball into the simmering syrup. Leave room for dumplings to rise, nearly double. Cover and let them gently simmer, for about 4–5 minutes. Lightly stir so that each dumpling is coated in the syrup reduction.

Mix the nutmeg and cinnamon sugar in a large bowl. Toss the glazed dumplings in the cinnamon sugar and serve drizzled with the hot syrup.

AEBLESKIVERS

Makes 14–20 aebleskivers

AEBLESKIVER PAN
20 COALS ON BOTTOM

4 eggs, separated
2 cups milk
¼ cup canola oil, plus
   more for cooking

1 tablespoon sugar
2 cups flour
½ teaspoon salt
1 teaspoon baking powder

In a medium bowl, beat egg yolks until lemon colored; stir in milk and oil and set aside. In a large bowl, sift sugar, flour, salt, and baking powder together. Add egg mixture into the dry ingredients, a little at a time, until the batter is evenly moistened. In another medium bowl, beat egg whites until they form stiff peaks then gently fold them into batter.

Preheat the pan by setting it on a trivet over all 20 coals. Use a pastry brush to generously oil each cup of the aebleskiver pan and fill ⅔ full with batter. Cook over all of the coals until edges of the aebleskivers are dry. This happens quickly and will take about 1 minute. Using two knitting needles,* press down on one side of the aebleskivers as you lift the other side to turn the aebleskivers in the cups. Only turn about a quarter turn. Do this until all sides are browned. Carefully watch your heat so that you don't burn the aebleskivers. Serve with syrup, jam, or simply sprinkle with powdered sugar.

VARIATION: Place small diced apples, shaken in cinnamon, on top of the unbaked batter in each cup. As you turn the aebleskiver, the apples will end up in the center.

Aebleskivers are a traditional Danish dessert. Knitting needles are the most recommended tool to use for turning. This just takes a little practice.

STRAWBERRY AND CREAM CREPES

Makes 12 crepes

10-INCH DUTCH OVEN
20 COALS ON BOTTOM

CREPES

2 cups milk

2 eggs, beaten

1¼ cups cornstarch

STRAWBERRY FILLING

8 ounces cream cheese, softened

⅓ cup whipped cream

½ teaspoon vanilla

½ cup powdered sugar

1 to 2 cups strawberries, sliced

CREPES

Place Dutch oven over all 20 coals and use oven like a skillet. In a large bowl, whisk milk and eggs together and then whisk in cornstarch. Mix well. The batter will be very thin. Pour about ¼ cup batter into hot oven. Tilt oven so that the batter is evenly dispersed over the bottom. Let cook for about 1 minute, the edges will dry and curl. Turn and brown the other side. Place on a plate to save until all crepes are cooked. Stir batter before making each crepe.

FILLING

In a medium bowl, beat cream cheese and whipped cream together and then add vanilla and powdered sugar. Generously spread cream cheese mixture on each crepe. Place a few strawberries on the crepe and roll up. Place seam side down on serving plate. You can also fold filled crepes into wedges for a serving variation. Garnish with strawberries.

✎ This is a gluten-free recipe.

CHOCOLATE CREPES

Makes 12 crepes

10-INCH DUTCH OVEN
20 COALS ON BOTTOM

3 teaspoons cocoa powder
2 teaspoons sugar
1¼ cups cornstarch
2 cups milk
2 eggs, beaten
Powdered sugar or cocoa powder

CREPES

Place Dutch oven over all 20 coals and use oven like a skillet. In a small bowl, combine cocoa powder, sugar, and cornstarch. In a large bowl, whisk milk and eggs together and then whisk in cornstarch mixture. Mix well. The batter will be very thin. Pour about ¼ cup batter into hot oven. Tilt oven so that the batter is evenly dispersed over the bottom. Let cook for about 1 minute, the edges will dry and curl. Turn and brown the other side. Place on a plate to save until all crepes are cooked. Stir batter before making each crepe.

Generously spread filling of choice on each crepe and roll up. Place seam side down on serving plate. Sprinkle with powdered sugar or cocoa powder.

FILLING OPTIONS

Dark chocolate chips and sliced bananas.
Dark chocolate chips and sliced strawberries.
Vanilla or strawberry yogurt with sliced strawberries.
Chocolate-hazelnut spread with berries and whipped cream.

This is a gluten-free recipe.

BREADS AND PASTRIES

BANANA BREAD 65

BANANA NUT BREAD 66

ALOHA BREAD 67

CRANBERRY ORANGE NUT BREAD 69

BAKING POWDER BISCUITS AND GRAVY 70

SAUSAGE BISCUIT BITES 72

SAUSAGE BREAKFAST BREAD 75

BRIOCHES DU CITRON 76

DOUGHNUTS 79

CINNAMON HAZELNUT BRAID 80

CINNAMON BREAD 83

CINNAMON ROLLS 84

SAUSAGE LOAF 87

APPLE CINNAMON BRAID 90

SCONES 92

LOUISIANA-STYLE BEIGNETS 93

DANISH PASTRY 94

BANANA BREAD

Serves 10

10-INCH DUTCH OVEN
7 COALS ON BOTTOM
13 COALS ON TOP
350 DEGREES

½ cup butter
¾ cup sugar
2 eggs
½ teaspoon salt
1½ teaspoons vanilla

4 ripe medium-size
  bananas, mashed
1¼ cups flour
1½ teaspoons baking soda
1 cup crushed walnuts
¼ cup buttermilk

In a large bowl, cream together the butter and sugar. Add eggs, salt, vanilla, and bananas; mix well. In a small bowl, combine flour and baking soda; add to the banana mixture along with the walnuts and buttermilk. Stir until just combined.

Grease and flour Dutch oven. Pour batter into oven. Cover and bake, using 7 coals underneath the oven and 13 coals on top, for 60–70 minutes or until bread tests done when a toothpick inserted in the center comes out clean. Cool in Dutch oven for about 10 minutes. Tip out of oven to finish cooling.

BANANA NUT BREAD

Serves 12

12-INCH DUTCH OVEN
9 COALS ON BOTTOM
18 COALS ON TOP
375 DEGREES

⅔ cup milk

2 tablespoons butter

¼ cup plus 1 tablespoon sugar, divided

1 tablespoon active dry yeast

1 egg

⅔ cup mashed banana

1 teaspoon salt

¼ cup pecan halves, chopped

1 teaspoon cinnamon

2½ to 3 cups flour

2 tablespoons butter, melted

Cinnamon sugar

In a small saucepan, heat milk and butter just enough to melt the butter, add 1 tablespoon sugar and yeast.

In a large bowl, beat together egg, banana, salt, remaining sugar, pecans, and cinnamon. Add milk mixture, blend well, and work in flour. Place on a floured surface and knead 8–10 minutes. Place bread dough in an oiled bowl and cover with plastic wrap. Let rise until double in size, about 1 hour.

Punch down dough and then shape into a loaf. Evenly split dough into thirds. Roll each third into equal-size ropes and braid; pinch ends to seal and tuck under. Pull top and bottom end of braid together to form a circle. Place in well-greased Dutch oven. Let rise for about 30 minutes. Brush loaf with melted butter and sprinkle with cinnamon sugar. Cover and bake, using 9 coals underneath the oven and 18 coals on top, for 35 minutes, or until lightly browned on top. Cool in Dutch oven for about 10 minutes. Tip out of oven to finish cooling.

ALOHA BREAD

Serves 15

12-INCH DUTCH OVEN
8 COALS ON BOTTOM
17 COALS ON TOP
375 DEGREES

3 cups flour

2 cups sugar

2 teaspoons baking soda

2 teaspoons vanilla

½ teaspoon salt

2 tablespoons grated orange zest

1 cup shredded coconut

1 (6-ounce) can crushed
pineapple, with liquid

2 cups grated carrots

3 eggs

½ cup butter

½ cup coconut oil or vegetable oil

1½ cups chopped walnuts

Sift together flour, sugar, and baking soda in a large bowl. Add all other ingredients and beat well.

Grease and flour Dutch oven. Place a parchment paper circle in the bottom of the Dutch oven. Grease the parchment paper. Pour batter into oven over paper. Cover and bake, using 8 coals underneath the oven and 17 coals on top, for 45 minutes or until a toothpick inserted in the center comes out clean. Remove lid and allow to cool for 15 minutes.

Replace the lid, and using heavy gloves, invert the oven, set on a trivet, and remove the oven off the lid. Peel paper from bottom of bread. Cool for another 15 minutes before serving.

CRANBERRY ORANGE NUT BREAD

Serves 15

10-INCH DUTCH OVEN
6 COALS ON BOTTOM
13 COALS ON TOP
350 DEGREES

2 cups flour

1 cup sugar

1½ teaspoons baking powder

1 teaspoon salt

½ teaspoon baking soda

¼ cup orange juice

1 egg, beaten

2 tablespoons shortening

1 tablespoon orange zest

1 cup cranberries, coarsely chopped (fresh or frozen)

½ cup walnuts

In large bowl, mix together the flour, sugar, baking powder, salt, and baking soda. Add orange juice, egg, shortening, and orange zest into the dry ingredients. Mix until blended. Stir in cranberries and nuts.

Pour batter into greased Dutch oven. Cover and bake, using 6 coals underneath the oven and 13 coals on top, for 55–60 minutes, or until a toothpick inserted in the center comes out clean. Cool in Dutch oven for 10 minutes and then tip bread out of oven to finish cooling.

BAKING POWDER BISCUITS AND GRAVY

Makes 16 biscuits

14-INCH DUTCH OVEN
14 COALS ON BOTTOM
26 COALS ON TOP
425 DEGREES

2 cups flour

1 teaspoon salt

4 teaspoons baking powder

1 teaspoon sugar

2 rounded tablespoons shortening

1 cup milk

Sift flour, salt, baking powder, and sugar into a medium bowl. Cut in shortening with a fork until mixture resembles coarse crumbs. Add milk all at once and mix just until dough follows fork around the bowl. Turn out on a floured surface and knead gently for about 30 seconds.

Roll into a ½-inch-thick rectangle. Using a 2–3-inch biscuit cutter or drinking glass, cut biscuits. Place closely together in bottom of ungreased Dutch oven. Press together dough scraps and cut more biscuits. Cover and bake, using 14 coals underneath the oven and 26 coals on top, for 12–15 minutes or until lightly browned. When biscuits are baked, remove from oven to a plate and cover with a towel while preparing gravy.

NOTE: *Coals will stay hot for 45 minutes. This recipe can be baked in a 12-inch oven with 11 coals under the Dutch oven and 22 on top. Bake 8 biscuits at a time.*

SAUSAGE GRAVY

Serves 12-16

14-INCH DUTCH OVEN
40 COALS ON BOTTOM

2 pounds ground sausage
½ cup flour
4 cups milk
Salt and pepper, to taste

After biscuits are finished baking, move all the coals under the Dutch oven and use oven like a skillet. Crumble and cook sausage until browned. Stir flour into oven with sausage and the fat until dissolved. Slowly stir in milk and cook until thick and bubbly. Season with salt and pepper. Serve over the biscuits.

COUNTRY GRAVY

Serves 16

14-INCH DUTCH OVEN
40 COALS ON BOTTOM

½ cup vegetable oil or butter
⅔ cup flour
4 cups milk or half-and-half
1 teaspoon seasoned salt
Pepper, to taste

After the biscuits are finished baking, move all the coals under the Dutch oven and use oven like a skillet. Heat oil or butter in bottom of the oven then whisk in flour and continue stirring until flour is dissolved. Slowly stir in milk and cook until thick and bubbly. Season with salt and pepper. Serve over the biscuits.

SAUSAGE BISCUIT BITES

Makes 16–20 biscuits

14-INCH DUTCH OVEN
14 COALS ON BOTTOM
26 COALS ON TOP
425 DEGREES

2⅔ cups flour

2 tablespoons sugar

1 teaspoon baking powder

½ teaspoon baking soda

½ teaspoon salt

½ cup shortening

1 tablespoon active dry yeast

¼ cup warm water (110 degrees)

1 cup buttermilk, room
  temperature

¾ pound ground hot sausage,
  cooked and crumbled

Melted butter

In a large bowl, mix together flour, sugar, baking powder, baking soda, and salt. Using a fork, cut in shortening until mixture resembles coarse crumbs. In a small bowl, dissolve yeast in warm water. Add buttermilk and then pour over dry ingredients and stir with a fork until the dry ingredients are moistened. Knead in sausage. Turn dough out onto a floured surface and knead lightly 3–4 times.

Roll dough out to a ½ inch thickness; cut with a 2-inch biscuit cutter or drinking glass. Place biscuits in ungreased Dutch oven. Press together dough scraps and cut more biscuits. Cover and bake, using 14 coals underneath the oven and 26 coals on top, for 12–15 minutes or until lightly browned. Brush tops with melted butter. Remove from oven to cooling rack and cover with a towel until ready to serve.

SAUSAGE BREAKFAST BREAD

Serves 6

10-INCH DUTCH OVEN
7 COALS ON BOTTOM
16 COALS ON TOP
375 DEGREES

2½ cups flour

½ teaspoon salt

1½ tablespoons sugar

3 tablespoons powdered milk

1 tablespoon rapid rise yeast

1¼ cup warm water (110 degrees)

1 egg, room temperature

1 pound ground sausage,
  cooked and crumbled

¼ teaspoon pepper

¼ teaspoon basil

In a large bowl, mix together flour, salt, sugar, powdered milk, and yeast. Stir to mix. Add water and egg. Beat vigorously for about 5 minutes. Add sausage, pepper, and basil. Mix until well combined. Spray Dutch oven with nonstick cooking spray and pour batter into Dutch oven. Let rise until double in size, about 30 minutes. Cover and bake, using 7 coals underneath the oven and 16 coals on top, for 30 minutes or until lightly browned. Allow to cool in oven for 10 minutes then tip out of oven for slicing.

BRIOCHES DU CITRON

Serves 10

12-INCH DEEP DUTCH OVEN
10 COALS ON BOTTOM
19 COALS ON TOP
400 DEGREES

BREAD DOUGH

1 tablespoon active dry yeast

2 tablespoons sugar

¾ cup warm water

1 egg, room temperature

2 tablespoons canola oil

½ cup plus 1 tablespoon milk

1½ teaspoons salt

⅓ cup potato flakes

3 to 4 cups flour

FILLING

½ cup butter, room temperature

1 cup sugar

3 tablespoons lemon zest

GLAZE, OPTIONAL

2½ cups powdered sugar

¼ cup butter, softened

3 tablespoons milk

1 teaspoon almond extract

1 cup toasted chopped almonds

BREAD DOUGH

In a small bowl, stir together yeast, sugar, and water. Let stand until foamy, about 10 minutes. In a large bowl, mix the egg, oil, milk, salt, and potato flakes. Add yeast mixture to egg mixture. Gradually add flour, working into a soft dough. Place dough on a lightly floured surface and knead for about 10 minutes. Put dough in a greased bowl, turning to coat the entire surface. Cover and let rise in warm area until double in size, about 1½ hours.

FILLING

In a small bowl, beat butter and sugar to blend well. Stir in lemon zest.

continued

GLAZE

In a medium bowl, beat all ingredients together, except for the almonds.

Roll dough out on generously floured surface to a 10 x 16-inch rectangle. Spread filling evenly over dough. Roll up dough, jelly-roll style. Cut into triangle wedges and place in greased Dutch oven with points in center. Set aside to rise until near double in size, about 30 minutes. Cover and bake, using 10 coals underneath the oven and 19 coals on top, for 30 minutes or until lightly browned. Glaze while still warm, if using. Sprinkle almonds on top of bread.

VARIATION: Use orange zest instead of lemon zest.

DOUGHNUTS

Makes 24 doughnuts

12-INCH DUTCH OVEN
24–27 COALS ON BOTTOM

DOUGHNUTS

1 tablespoon active dry yeast
¾ cup warm water, divided
½ cup milk, warmed
   (110 degrees)
2 tablespoons shortening, melted
¼ cup sugar
1½ teaspoons salt
1 egg, beaten

1 teaspoon nutmeg
3¾ cups sifted flour
Vegetable oil 3–4 inches
   deep in Dutch oven

GLAZE

2½ cups powdered sugar
¼ cup butter, softened
3 tablespoons milk
1 teaspoon almond extract

DOUGHNUTS

In a large bowl, dissolve yeast in ¼ cup water. Let stand for 5 minutes. In a small bowl, combine the remaining water, milk, shortening, sugar, salt, egg, and nutmeg. Mix well and add flour, a little at a time, until you have a soft dough. Place in a greased bowl, turning to grease top, cover, and place in refrigerator for 2–3 hours or overnight.

Roll out on a lightly floured surface to ¼ inch thick and cut with a floured doughnut cutter. Let rise in a warm place until double in size, about 1 hour.

Starting with 24 coals, heat the oil in the Dutch oven, adding more coals if needed, so the oil temperature reaches 375–400 degrees.

Fry 2–3 doughnuts at a time, turning once to brown both sides. Drain on paper towels and sprinkle with sugar or glaze.

GLAZE

In a medium bowl, combine ingredients until smooth.

Don't forget to fry some doughnut holes!

CINNAMON HAZELNUT BRAID

Serves 20

OVAL ROASTER DUTCH OVEN*
10 COALS ON BOTTOM
20 COALS ON TOP
375 DEGREES

BREAD DOUGH

1 cup milk
⅓ cup butter
⅓ cup sugar
2 tablespoons active dry yeast
4 to 4½ cups flour, divided
2 teaspoons salt
2 teaspoons grated orange zest
2 eggs

FILLING

1 cup powdered sugar
⅓ cup butter, softened
1 teaspoon cinnamon
1 cup hazelnuts, ground

GLAZE

3 tablespoons sugar
¼ cup orange juice

BREAD DOUGH

In a small saucepan, warm milk and butter just enough to melt butter. Add sugar and yeast. In a large bowl, combine 2 cups flour, salt, and orange zest and mix well. When yeast is foamy, add to flour mixture. Add eggs and beat until well mixed. Add additional flour and knead until you have a soft dough, about 10 minutes. Place dough in a greased bowl, cover with plastic wrap, and let rise until double in size, about 1 hour.

FILLING

In a small bowl, cream together powdered sugar, butter, and cinnamon. Set aside.

GLAZE

In another small bowl, blend glaze ingredients. Set aside.

After bread dough has risen, punch down and turn dough out on a floured surface. Divide into 3 equal portions. Roll each portion out into a 6 x 12-inch rectangle. Spread with a third of the butter and sugar mixture and sprinkle with hazelnuts. Roll up jelly-roll style, starting with the long side; pinch seams to seal.

Place the 3 ropes seam side down and braid; pinch ends to seal and tuck under. Place in greased Dutch oven, cover, and let rise until double in size, about 45 minutes. Cover and bake, using 10 coals underneath the oven and 20 coals on top, for 25–30 minutes. Brush with glaze and bake an additional 3–5 minutes. Bread should be golden brown. Remove from hot oven and cool on wire racks.

Since an oval roaster Dutch oven does not have legs, place oven on 2 trivets, one at each end, and place coals underneath. Use heavy-duty aluminum foil to make a boat to hold the coals on the lid.

CINNAMON BREAD

Serves 12

12-INCH DUTCH OVEN
8 COALS ON BOTTOM
17 COALS ON TOP
350 DEGREES

BREAD DOUGH

1 tablespoon rapid rise yeast

¾ teaspoon salt

3 cups flour

¼ teaspoon nutmeg

½ tablespoon cinnamon

1½ tablespoons sugar

1½ tablespoons powdered milk

¾ cup warm water (110 degrees)

½ teaspoon vanilla

½ cup butter, melted

FILLING

3 tablespoons brown sugar

1¼ teaspoons cinnamon

¼ teaspoon nutmeg

½ cup raisins or nuts, optional

BREAD DOUGH

In a large bowl, combine yeast, salt, flour, nutmeg, cinnamon, sugar, powdered milk, water, vanilla, and butter. Knead for 10 minutes on a lightly floured surface. Place in a greased bowl and turn to grease top. Cover and let rise until double in size, about 1 hour. Punch down then shape into a 6 x 16-inch rectangle.

FILLING

Combine ingredients in a small bowl.

Spread filling over rectangle and press into dough with back of spoon. Roll from the long edge forming a long rope; pinch to seal edge. Coil and place in greased Dutch oven. Cover and bake, using 8 coals underneath the oven and 17 coals on top, for 35 minutes or until lightly browned.

VARIATION: Drizzle with Glaze (page 84) while still warm.

CINNAMON ROLLS

Serves 12

14-INCH DUTCH OVEN
12 COALS ON BOTTOM
24 COALS ON TOP
400 DEGREES

BREAD DOUGH

1 tablespoon active dry yeast
1⅓ cups warm water
 (110 degrees)
¼ cup sugar
¼ cup canola oil
1 egg, room temperature
1 teaspoon salt
4 to 5 cups flour

FILLING

½ cup butter, room temperature
¾ cup sugar
3 tablespoons cinnamon

GLAZE, OPTIONAL

1½ cups powdered sugar
¼ cup butter, softened
3 tablespoons milk
1 teaspoon vanilla

BREAD DOUGH

In a large bowl, stir together yeast, water, and sugar. Let stand until foamy, about 5 minutes. Stir oil, egg, and salt into mixture. Add flour, ½ cup at a time, stirring until mixed in and smooth. Place dough on a lightly floured surface and knead, for about 10 minutes. Grease a large bowl and add dough, turning once to coat entire surface. Cover and let rise in a warm place until double in size, about 1½ hours.

FILLING

In a small bowl, beat butter, sugar, and cinnamon. Set aside.

continued

GLAZE

In a small bowl, beat powdered sugar, butter, milk, and vanilla together. Set aside.

Roll dough out on generously floured surface to make a 10 x 16-inch rectangle. Spread filling evenly over dough. Roll up dough, jelly-roll style. Cut into 12 slices. Place rolls into greased Dutch oven, 8 rolls around edge of the oven and 4 in the center. Cover and set aside to rise until double in size, about 1 hour. Cover and bake, using 12 coals underneath the oven and 24 coals on top, for 30 minutes, or until lightly browned. When done, tip bread out of oven and glaze while still warm, if using.

SAUSAGE LOAF

Serves 6–8

OVAL ROASTER DUTCH OVEN*
12 COALS ON BOTTOM
24 COALS ON TOP
400 DEGREES

1 recipe bread dough from
  Cinnamon Rolls (page 84)

FILLING

½ pound ground Italian sausage
½ yellow onion, chopped
¼ cup diced celery
1 teaspoon minced garlic

1 cup peeled and diced
  Granny Smith apple
1 tablespoon butter
½ cup cooked rice (white or wild)
1 cup grated Parmesan
  cheese, divided
Egg wash of 1 egg beaten
  into 1 tablespoon water

FILLING

The filling is best if prepared the day before needed and refrigerated to let the flavors blend. In a large skillet, crumble sausage and brown; remove sausage from skillet and drain grease. In the same skillet, sauté onion, celery, garlic, and apple in butter until onion becomes translucent, 3–5 minutes. Stir into cooked sausage. Add rice and half of the cheese.

Roll dough out on a generously floured surface to make a 12 x 16-inch rectangle. Spread filling down the center third of the rectangle. Fringe outer thirds of the dough into ¾-inch-wide slices. Fold top edge of dough over the top and alternately pull over each fringed slice of dough. This will braid your dough over the filling. Tuck last end under the loaf. Place loaf into greased Dutch oven. Set aside to rise until double in size, about 30 minutes.

continued

Carefully brush loaf with egg wash. Sprinkle with remaining cheese. Cover and bake, using 12 coals underneath the oven and 24 coals on top, for 30–40 minutes or until lightly browned.

Since an oval roaster Dutch oven does not have legs, place oven on 2 trivets, one at each end, and place coals underneath. Use heavy-duty aluminum foil to make a boat to hold the coals on the lid.

APPLE CINNAMON BRAID

Serves 6–8

OVAL ROASTER DUTCH OVEN*
12 COALS ON BOTTOM
24 COALS ON TOP
400 DEGREES

1 recipe Cinnamon Rolls (page 84)
1 can (21 ounces) apple pie filling
    added to the filling

Prepare dough following the Cinnamon Rolls recipe and let rise until double in size, about 1 hour. Roll dough out on a generously floured surface to make a 12 x 16-inch rectangle. Spread filling down the center third of the rectangle. Fringe the outer thirds of the dough into ½-inch-wide slices. Fold top edge of dough over the top end and alternately pull over each fringed slice of dough. This will braid your dough over the filling. Tuck last end under the loaf. Place loaf into greased Dutch oven. Set aside to rise until double in size, about 30 minutes.

Cover and bake, using 12 coals underneath the oven and 24 coals on top, for 30 minutes, or until lightly browned. When done, tip bread out of oven and glaze while still warm.

*Since an oval roaster Dutch oven does not have legs, place oven on 2 trivets, one at each end, and place coals underneath. Use heavy-duty aluminum foil to make a boat to hold the coals on the lid.

SCONES

Makes 12 scones

12-inch Dutch oven
24–27 coals on bottom

1 tablespoon active dry yeast	1½ teaspoons salt
1¼ cups warm water, divided	1 egg, beaten
⅓ cup powdered milk	2½ cups flour
¼ cup shortening, melted	Vegetable oil 1 inch deep
¼ cup sugar	in Dutch oven

In a small bowl, sprinkle yeast over ¼ cup warm water and allow to foam. Combine remaining water, powdered milk, shortening, sugar, salt, egg, and flour in a medium bowl. Add yeast mixture. Work until you have a soft dough. Turn out onto a floured surface and knead for about 10 minutes. Dough should be soft and elastic. Place in an oiled bowl and cover with a kitchen towel. Keep warm and allow to rise until double in size, about 1 hour.

Starting with 24 coals, heat the oil in the Dutch oven, adding more coals if needed so the oil reaches 375–400 degrees.

Knead dough to press out any air pockets. Roll to ¼ inch thick and allow dough to relax for 1 minute before cutting to desired shape. You can also just stretch a handful of dough into a 4-inch flat circle. Drop into hot oil and fry until brown on bottom. Turn scone to brown the other side. Remove from oven and drain on paper towels. Continue to fry dough. Serve with butter and honey, syrup, or jam.

LOUISIANA–STYLE BEIGNETS

Makes 30 beignets

12-INCH DUTCH OVEN
24–27 COALS ON BOTTOM

1 tablespoon dry yeast
3 tablespoons warm
   water (110 degrees)
¾ cup milk, warmed
   (110 degrees)
¼ cup sugar
¼ cup shortening, melted

1 teaspoon salt
1 egg, beaten
2½ to 3 cups flour
Vegetable oil 3 inches
   deep in Dutch oven
Powdered sugar

In a large bowl, dissolve yeast in water. In a small bowl, stir together milk, sugar, shortening, and salt. Add milk mixture, egg, and 2 cups flour to yeast mixture. Mix well. Stir in enough remaining flour to make a soft dough. Turn dough out onto a floured surface and knead for about 8–10 minutes, until smooth and elastic. Place into a well-greased bowl and turn to grease top. Cover and let rise in a warm place for about 1 hour.

Punch down dough and turn out onto a floured surface. Roll out dough into a 10 x 12-inch rectangle; cut into 2-inch squares. Place on a floured surface, cover, and let rise in a warm place for about 30 minutes.

Starting with 24 coals, heat the oil in the Dutch oven, adding more coals if needed so the oil reaches 375–400 degrees.

Drop in 5–6 beignets at a time and cook for 1 minute on each side or until golden brown. Drain on paper towels; sprinkle with powdered sugar.

DANISH PASTRY

Makes 24 pastries

14-inch Dutch oven
12 coals on bottom
22 coals on top
375 degrees

½ cup warm water

2 tablespoons active dry yeast

¾ cup milk, room temperature

½ cup sugar

1½ teaspoons salt

¼ cup butter, melted and cooled

2 eggs

1½ teaspoons lemon zest

3½ cups flour, divided

2 tablespoons cornstarch

1½ cups butter, softened

½ cup raspberry jelly

Sugar

In a small bowl, dissolve yeast in warm water and set aside until foamy. In a large bowl, combine milk, sugar, salt, and melted butter. Add yeast into mixture.

In a small bowl, beat eggs yolks and 1 egg white; reserve remaining egg white until later. Add eggs and lemon zest to yeast mixture. Add 1 cup flour and mix really well. Combine cornstarch with remaining flour; stir into batter until just mixed. Chill for 1 hour.

Spread softened butter on waxed paper in a 10 x 12-inch rectangle. Place on a tray and chill 1 hour.

Roll chilled dough into a 12 x 16-inch rectangle. Place wax paper with chilled butter, butter side down, over ⅔ of rolled out dough. Remove wax paper. Fold uncovered third of dough over middle section then fold remaining third toward middle. Give dough a quarter turn and roll into a 12 x 16-inch rectangle. Fold into thirds as above and turn and roll into a 12 x 16-inch rectangle. Place on tray and chill for 1 hour. Repeat procedure of rolling, folding, turning, and chilling 2 times. Then refrigerate overnight. This process incorporates the butter into layers within the dough so that when baking the butter melts and makes the dough flaky.

Shape half of the dough at a time, refrigerating the other half. Roll the dough half into a 9 x 12-inch rectangle. Cut the dough into 3-inch squares. Place ½ teaspoon jelly in the center of each square and fold opposite corners to overlap ½ inch in the center over jelly. Place in greased Dutch oven. Brush pastries with reserved egg white and sprinkle with sugar.

Cover and bake, using 12 coals underneath the oven and 22 coals on top, for 15–20 minutes. While the first pastries are baking, prepare second half of pastry. When the pastries are baked, remove them from the oven to a cooling rack. Remove oven from heat while loading second batch of pastries. Return oven to heat to bake.

BREAKFAST CASSEROLES

BAKED OMELET SQUARES 97

MOCK SOUFFLÉ 99

MICHAEL'S LAYERED MOUNTAIN MAN 100

FAVORITE MOUNTAIN MAN BREAKFAST 102

CORNBREAD BREAKFAST CASSEROLE 103

QUICK BREAKFAST CASSEROLE 106

BRUNCH EGG CASSEROLE 107

SCRAMBLED EGG CASSEROLE 108

SAUSAGE POTATO CASSEROLE 111

PENNSYLVANIA DUTCH CASSEROLE 112

RICE AND SAUSAGE ESPECIAL 113

BAKED OMELET SQUARES

Serves 8

12-INCH DUTCH OVEN
9 COALS ON BOTTOM
18 COALS ON TOP
375 DEGREES

2 tablespoons butter

1 small onion, chopped

1½ cups grated cheddar cheese

1 (12-ounce) can sliced
  mushrooms

1 (6-ounce) can sliced black olives

2 cups chopped cooked ham

12 eggs, beaten

½ cup milk

½ teaspoon salt

½ teaspoon pepper

Place Dutch oven over all 27 coals and use oven like a skillet. Melt the butter in bottom of the Dutch oven and then cook onion until tender. Spread cheese in the bottom of the oven with the onions. Then layer the mushrooms, olives, and ham.

In a large bowl, combine the eggs with milk and season with salt and pepper. Pour over ingredients in the Dutch oven. Do not stir. Cover and bake, using 9 coals underneath the oven and 18 coals on top, for 30 minutes or until mixture is set in the center. Allow to cool slightly and cut into squares.

❧ This is a gluten-free recipe.

MOCK SOUFFLE

Serves 10-12

12-INCH DUTCH OVEN
9 COALS ON BOTTOM
14 COALS ON TOP
350 DEGREES

Enough butter to coat oven
14 slices bread, crusts
   removed and cubed
1 cup small-dice cooked ham
2 cups grated cheddar cheese

5 eggs
4 cups milk
½ teaspoon dry mustard
½ teaspoon salt
⅛ teaspoon pepper

Coat the oven with butter. Layer half of the bread in bottom of oven. Cover with half the ham and half the cheese. Top with the remaining bread, followed with remaining ham and cheese.

In a large bowl, beat eggs; add milk and seasonings. Pour over top of all layers. Cover with plastic wrap and refrigerate for at least 8 hours or overnight.

When ready to cook, remove plastic wrap, and cover and bake, using 9 coals underneath the oven and 14 coals on top, for 1 hour or until knife inserted in center comes out clean.

MICHAEL'S LAYERED MOUNTAIN MAN

Serves 18

14-INCH DUTCH OVEN
8 COALS ON BOTTOM
20 COALS ON TOP
350 DEGREES

1 pound ground sausage,
  crumbled

1 pound bacon, diced

1 medium yellow onion, diced

1 red bell pepper, diced

1 yellow bell pepper, diced

1 (32-ounce) bag frozen
  diced potatoes

1 tablespoon steak
  seasoning or rub

12 eggs, beaten

2 cups grated sharp
  cheddar cheese

Place Dutch oven over all 28 coals and use oven like a skillet. Brown sausage and remove from Dutch oven; set aside. Brown the bacon and then add onion and cook until translucent. Add bell peppers and cook for 10 minutes. Add potatoes and seasoning; cook, stirring occasionally, until potatoes start to brown. Compress potato mixture to make a firm "cake" in the bottom of the oven. Pour eggs over the potatoes. Do not stir in eggs; they should sit mostly on top of the potatoes.

Cover and move 20 coals to the lid. Cook until eggs are nearly set, 7–10 minutes. Layer the sausage over the eggs and continue cooking. When the eggs are completely cooked, sprinkle cheese over the sausage and replace the lid to melt the cheese.

♥ This is a gluten-free recipe.

FAVORITE MOUNTAIN MAN BREAKFAST

Serves 12

12-INCH DUTCH OVEN
8 COALS ON BOTTOM
16 COALS ON TOP
350 DEGREES

½ pound bacon, diced
½ pound ground sage
  sausage, crumbled
1 medium onion, diced

1 (32-ounce) bag hash
  brown potatoes
12 eggs
½ pound extra sharp
  cheddar cheese, grated

Place Dutch oven over all 24 coals and use oven like a skillet. Brown bacon and sausage in bottom of oven then add onion and cook until translucent. Stir in the potatoes and cover. Move 16 coals to the lid. Stir occasionally to brown potatoes, about 15–20 minutes.

In a large bowl, beat the eggs and then pour over the potatoes. Cover and cook, using the same coals, until eggs start to set, about 10–15 minutes. Sprinkle cheese over egg mixture, cover, and continue heating until eggs are completely set and cheese is melted. Slice and serve.

This is a gluten-free recipe.

CORNBREAD BREAKFAST CASSEROLE

Serves 8

2 (12-INCH) DUTCH OVENS
10 COALS ON BOTTOM
19 COALS ON TOP
400 DEGREES

CRUST

½ teaspoon baking soda

1 cup buttermilk

4 tablespoons melted butter

1 cup cornmeal

¼ cup sugar

½ teaspoon salt

1 egg, beaten

1 (14.5-ounce) can whole
  kernel corn, drained

2 tablespoons diced green
  chiles, drained

FILLING

1 pound ground sausage

1 red bell pepper, chopped

1 onion (yellow or red), chopped

2 cloves garlic, minced

1 teaspoon cumin

EGGS

5 eggs, beaten

1 cup milk

1 teaspoon each salt and pepper

1 cup grated cheddar cheese

CRUST

Place Dutch oven over 10 coals and place lid on oven with 19 coals on top. Let oven preheat while mixing cornbread. Add baking soda to the buttermilk and let it sit while you assemble remaining crust ingredients. In a large bowl, combine butter, cornmeal, sugar, salt, egg, corn, and chiles and mix well. Add in buttermilk. Pour into hot Dutch oven and bake for 15–18 minutes. Remove Dutch oven from heat.

continued

FILLING

Place the second Dutch oven over all 29 coals and use oven like a skillet. Brown sausage with onion and red bell pepper. Stir in garlic and cumin. Layer filling over top of the cornbread crust.

EGGS

In a large bowl, combine eggs, milk, salt, and pepper. Pour the egg mixture over the filling. Cover and bake, using 4 coals underneath the oven and 19 coals on top, for 35–40 minutes. Because you have already cooked the corn bread, most of the heat will be required on top. During last 5 minutes, sprinkle with cheese and allow cheese to melt.

❧ This is a gluten-free recipe.

QUICK BREAKFAST CASSEROLE

Serves 8

12-INCH DUTCH OVEN
10 COALS ON BOTTOM
19 COALS ON TOP
400 DEGREES

1 (8-ounce) can crescent rolls

½ to 1 pound ground sausage, browned and drained

1 cup grated mozzarella cheese

5 eggs

¼ cup milk

1 teaspoon oregano or rosemary

½ teaspoon salt

¼ teaspoon pepper

Spread the crescent rolls in the bottom of Dutch oven, pressing the seams together. Scatter the sausage and cheese on rolls.

In a medium bowl, whisk eggs, milk, oregano, salt, and pepper. Pour on top of the sausage and cheese. Cover and bake, using 10 coals underneath the oven and 19 coals on top, for 18–20 minutes.

BRUNCH EGG CASSEROLE

Serves 8–10

12-INCH DUTCH OVEN
8 COALS ON BOTTOM
16 COALS ON TOP
350 DEGREES

2 cups unseasoned croutons

1 cup grated sharp
cheddar cheese

4 to 5 eggs, beaten

2 cups milk

½ teaspoon dry mustard

⅛ teaspoon onion powder

½ teaspoon salt

Dash of pepper

4 to 6 slices bacon, cooked
and crumbled

Place croutons and cheese in bottom of greased oven. In a large bowl, combine eggs, milk, and seasonings; whisk together. Pour over cheese in oven. Sprinkle with bacon. Cover and bake, using 8 coals underneath the oven and 16 coals on top, for 30–35 minutes or until eggs are set.

SCRAMBLED EGG CASSEROLE

Serves 8

12-INCH DUTCH OVEN
6 COALS ON BOTTOM
18 COALS ON TOP
350 DEGREES

2 tablespoons butter

1/2 cup sliced green onions

12 eggs

1/2 cup half-and-half

1 1/2 cups diced cooked ham

1 (10.75-ounce) can cream
   of mushroom soup

1 cup grated cheddar cheese

Place Dutch oven over all 24 coals and use oven like a skillet. Melt butter in oven and sauté onions until tender.

In a large bowl, beat eggs and then stir in half-and-half. Pour egg mixture into oven with onions. Stir gently and add ham. Cook eggs, stirring only a little, so the eggs are of a good size. Stirring too much will break them into smaller pieces. Pour soup evenly over the top of the eggs.

Cover and bake, using 6 coals underneath the oven and 18 coals on top, for 20 minutes. Sprinkle cheese over casserole and bake an additional 10 minutes.

VARIATION: You can substitute sausage, bacon, or Canadian bacon for the ham.

❧ This is a gluten-free recipe.

SAUSAGE POTATO CASSEROLE

Serves 8–10

12-INCH DUTCH OVEN
8 COALS ON BOTTOM
16 COALS ON TOP
350 DEGREES

1 cup mayonnaise
1 cup sour cream
1 medium onion, chopped
½ teaspoon seasoned salt

1 (1-pound 14-ounce) bag frozen shredded hash brown potatoes
1 pound smoked sausage, cut into ¼-inch slices

Mix all ingredients together in a large bowl. Spray Dutch oven with nonstick cooking spray and pour mixed ingredients into oven. Cover and bake, using 8 coals underneath the oven and 16 coals on top, for 45 minutes.

❧ This is a gluten-free recipe.

PENNSYLVANIA DUTCH CASSEROLE

Serves 8-10

12-INCH DUTCH OVEN
8 COALS ON BOTTOM
16 COALS ON TOP
350 DEGREES

1 pound bacon, diced

1 medium onion, chopped

6 eggs, beaten

1 cup frozen hash brown
potatoes, thawed

2 cups grated cheddar cheese

1½ cups small curd
cottage cheese

1¼ cups grated Swiss cheese

Place Dutch oven over all 24 coals and use oven like a skillet. Cook bacon and onion until bacon is crisp; remove from oven into a large bowl.

Wipe out excess bacon grease from oven. Add remaining ingredients to bacon and mix well. Pour into Dutch oven. Cover and bake, using 8 coals underneath the oven and 16 coals on top, for 35-40 minutes or until a knife inserted in the center comes out clean. Let set for 10 minutes before serving.

This is a gluten-free recipe.

RICE AND SAUSAGE ESPECIAL

Serves 4

10-INCH DUTCH OVEN
6 COALS ON BOTTOM
14 COALS ON TOP
350 DEGREES

1 pound ground hot sausage
½ cup diced celery
½ cup diced onion
½ cup diced green bell pepper

2 cups cooked rice
½ (10.75-ounce) can
   chicken gumbo soup
½ cup water

Place Dutch oven over all 20 coals and use oven like a skillet. Cook sausage, celery, onion, and bell pepper until sausage is browned and vegetables are softened. Remove from Dutch oven into a medium bowl and set aside.

Wipe out excess fat from bottom of oven. Place rice in bottom of oven. Layer the sausage and vegetables over the rice. Mix water and soup together and pour over rice and sausage. Cover and bake, using 6 coals underneath the oven and 14 coals on top, for 30 minutes or until heated through.

FAMILY FAVORITES

BREAD PUDDING 115

RICE PUDDING 116

OLD-FASHIONED BREAD PUDDING 119

WELSH RAREBIT 120

APPLE PUDDING 122

BREAD PUDDING

Serves 8

10-INCH DUTCH OVEN
7 COALS ON BOTTOM
13 COALS ON TOP
350 DEGREES

Butter	¼ teaspoon salt
2 eggs	Pinch of nutmeg
2 cups milk	½ teaspoon cinnamon
1 cup sugar	3 to 4 slices day old bread, cubed
1 teaspoon vanilla	½ cup raisins

Butter bottom and sides of Dutch oven.

In a medium bowl, beat eggs and then add milk, sugar, vanilla, salt, nutmeg, and cinnamon. Place bread cubes into Dutch oven and pour egg mixture over bread. Let stand 30 minutes and then gently stir in raisins before baking. Cover and bake, using 7 coals underneath the oven and 13 coals on top, for 30 minutes or until firm.

VARIATIONS: Coconut, diced apple, and nuts may be added. Try various flavorings like almond or black walnut—add ½ teaspoon flavoring and only ½ teaspoon vanilla.

RICE PUDDING

Serves 8

10-INCH DUTCH OVEN
7 COALS ON BOTTOM
13 COALS ON TOP
350 DEGREES

½ cup raisins

1 cup water

2 eggs

1 cup sugar

1 teaspoon cinnamon

1 teaspoon vanilla

Pinch of salt

4 cups milk, divided

1 cup uncooked rice

3 tablespoons butter

Place raisins in a small bowl to soak in water an hour or so before baking. In a large bowl, beat eggs until fluffy. Add sugar, cinnamon, vanilla, salt, and 1 cup of milk. Mix well until sugar is dissolved. Drain raisins and add to mixture with remaining milk and rice. Pour into Dutch oven. Dot top of pudding with butter. Cover and bake, using 7 coals underneath the oven and 13 coals on top, for 30–40 minutes or until pudding is firm.

This is a gluten-free recipe.

OLD-FASHIONED BREAD PUDDING

Serves 8-10

12-INCH DUTCH OVEN
7 COALS ON BOTTOM
18 COALS ON TOP
350 DEGREES

1 (16-ounce) loaf day old
French bread, cubed

2 (12-ounce) cans evaporated milk

1 cup water

6 eggs, lightly beaten

1 (8-ounce) can crushed
pineapple, drained

1 large Granny Smith
apple, grated

1½ cups sugar

1 cup chopped dates

5 tablespoons vanilla

¼ cup butter, diced and softened

Whipped cream

In a large bowl, combine bread, milk, and water. Stir in eggs, blending well. Add pineapple, apple, sugar, dates, and vanilla. Spray inside of Dutch oven with nonstick cooking spray and pour mixture into oven. Cover and bake, using 7 coals underneath the oven and 18 coals on top, for 35-40 minutes or until firm. Serve with a dollop of whipped cream.

WELSH RAREBIT

Serves 6–8

10-INCH DUTCH OVEN
10 COALS ON BOTTOM

2 tablespoons butter

4 cups grated sharp
  cheddar cheese

2 eggs

1 teaspoon Worcestershire sauce

½ teaspoon dry mustard

Pinch of cayenne pepper

½ cup half-and-half

English muffins or toast

Place Dutch oven over all 10 coals and use as a saucepan.

In bottom of Dutch oven, melt the butter. Add cheese, a little at a time, and stir after each addition until all the cheese is melted. In a small bowl, beat eggs and then add Worcestershire sauce, mustard, and cayenne pepper; stir in half-and-half. Stir egg mixture into cheese. Cook until thickened. Serve over English muffin halves or toasted bread.

APPLE PUDDING

Serves 6

10-INCH DUTCH OVEN
8 COALS ON BOTTOM
17 COALS ON TOP
350 DEGREES

1 cup sugar
2 cups grated apples
1 egg
1/4 cup melted butter
1 cup flour

1/2 teaspoon salt
1/2 teaspoon cinnamon
1/2 teaspoon cloves
1 teaspoon baking soda

In a small bowl, pour sugar over apples and set aside. In a large bowl, beat egg and butter together. Add apples and stir in remaining ingredients. Pour into greased Dutch oven. Cover and bake, using 8 coals underneath the oven and 17 coals on top, for 30–40 minutes or until firm.

INDEX

A

Aebleskivers, 59
almond, in Brioches du Citron, 76
Aloha Bread, 67
apple:
Apple Cinnamon Braid, 90
Apple Pudding, 122
Fluffy Apple Pancake, 55
Old-Fashioned Bread
Pudding, 119
Sausage Loaf, 87
applesauce, in German
Potato Pancakes, 38

B

bacon:
Brunch Egg Casserole, 107
Classic Quiche Lorraine, 26
Cowboy Creamies, 35
Denver Omelet, 19
Dutch Oven Sparkling
Potatoes, 43
Favorite Mountain Man
Breakfast, 102
Michael's Layered
Mountain Man, 100
Pennsylvania Dutch
Casserole, 112
Potato Spears, 40
Baked Omelet Squares, 97
Baking Powder Biscuits
and Gravy, 70
Banana Bread, 65
Banana Nut Bread, 66
Basic Omelet, The, 17
Beignets, Louisiana-Style, 93
bell pepper:
Cornbread Breakfast
Casserole, 103
Denver Omelet, 19
Firehouse Hash, 44
Italian Sausage Omelet, 20
Michael's Layered
Mountain Man, 100
Rice and Sausage Especial, 113

Spanish Scrambled Eggs, 23
Sunrise Potatoes, 39
berries, in Fruit Filling, 53
biscuit:
Baking Powder Biscuits
and Gravy, 70
Sausage Biscuit Bites, 72
Biscuit tips, 15
Blue Cheese Quiche, 28
braid:
Apple Cinnamon Braid, 90
Cinnamon Hazelnut Braid, 80
bread:
Aloha Bread, 67
Banana Bread, 65
Banana Nut Bread, 66
Bread Pudding, 115
Cinnamon Bread, 83
Cranberry Orange
Nut Bread, 69
in French Toast Soufflé, 56
in Mock Soufflé, 99
in Picture Perfect Eggs
and Toast, 25
Old-Fashioned Bread
Pudding, 119
Sausage Breakfast Bread, 75
Bread tips, 15
breakfast:
Breakfast Burritos, 36
Breakfast Hash, 45
Cornbread Breakfast
Casserole, 103
Favorite Mountain Man
Breakfast, 102
Quick Breakfast Casserole, 106
Sausage Breakfast Bread, 75
Brioches du Citron, 76
Brunch Egg Casserole, 107
Burritos, Breakfast, 36
buttermilk:
Banana Bread, 65
Cornbread Breakfast
Casserole, 103
Sausage Biscuit Bites, 72

C

Canadian bacon, in Eggs
Benedict, 31
carrot, in Aloha Bread, 67
casserole:
Brunch Egg Casserole, 107
Cornbread Breakfast
Casserole, 103
Pennsylvania Dutch
Casserole, 112
Quick Breakfast Casserole, 106
Sausage Potato Casserole, 111
Scrambled Egg Casserole, 108
celery:
Rice and Sausage Especial, 113
Sausage Loaf, 87
cheese:
blue, in Blue Cheese Quiche, 28
cheddar:
Baked Omelet Squares, 97
Basic Omelet, The, 17
Breakfast Burritos, 36
Brunch Egg Casserole, 107
Cornbread Breakfast
Casserole, 103
Cowboy Creamies, 35
Denver Omelet, 19
Dutch Oven Sparkling
Potatoes, 43
Favorite Mountain Man
Breakfast, 102
Firehouse Hash, 44
Mock Soufflé, 99
Michael's Layered
Mountain Man, 100
Pennsylvania Dutch
Casserole, 112
Scrambled Egg
Casserole, 108
Spanish Scrambled Eggs, 23
Welsh Rarebit, 120
cottage:
Easy Crust-less Quiche, 30
Pennsylvania Dutch
Casserole, 112

cheese (continued)
cream:
Blue Cheese Quiche, 28
French Toast Soufflé, 56
Fruit Filling, 53
Strawberry Filling, 61
mozzarella:
Easy Crust-less Quiche, 30
Quick Breakfast
Casserole, 106
Parmesan:
Breakfast Hash, 45
Easy Crust-less Quiche, 30
Picture Perfect Eggs
and Toast, 25
Sausage Loaf, 87
Swiss, in Pennsylvania
Dutch Casserole, 112
chile:
Breakfast Burritos, 36
Cornbread Breakfast
Casserole, 103
chocolate:
Chocolate Crepes, 62
chocolate-hazelnut spread,
in Stuffed Pancakes, 53
cinnamon:
Apple Cinnamon Braid, 90
Cinnamon Bread, 83
Cinnamon Hazelnut Braid, 80
Cinnamon Rolls, 84
Classic Quiche Lorraine, 26
Cleaning your Dutch oven, 12
coconut, in Aloha Bread, 67
corn, in Cornbread Breakfast
Casserole, 103
Cornbread Breakfast
Casserole, 103
Country Gravy, 71
Cowboy Creamies, 35
Cranberry Orange Nut Bread, 69
Crepes, Chocolate, 62
Crepes, Strawberry and Cream, 61
crescent rolls, in Quick
Breakfast Casserole, 106
croissant rolls, in French
Toast Dumplings, 58
croutons, in Brunch Egg
Casserole, 107

D
Danish Pastry, 94
date, in Old-Fashioned
Bread Pudding, 119
Denver Omelet, 19
Doughnuts, 79
Dumplings, French Toast, 58
Dutch oven heat control, 8
Dutch Oven Sparkling
Potatoes, 43

E
Easy Crust-less Quiche, 30
egg:
Aebleskivers, 59
Aloha Bread, 67
Apple Pudding, 122
Baked Omelet Squares, 97
Banana Bread, 65
Banana Nut Bread, 66
Basic Omelet, The, 17
Blue Cheese Quiche, 28
Bread Pudding, 115
Breakfast Burritos, 36
Breakfast Hash, 45
Brunch Egg Casserole, 107
Chocolate Crepes, 62
Cinnamon Hazelnut Braid, 8
Cinnamon Rolls, 84
Classic Quiche Lorraine, 26
Cornbread Breakfast
Casserole, 103
Cranberry Orange
Nut Bread, 69
Danish Pastry, 94
Denver Omelet, 19
Doughnuts, 79
Easy Crust-less Quiche, 30
Eggs Benedict, 31
Favorite Mountain Man
Breakfast, 102
Fluffy Apple Pancake, 55
French Toast Soufflé, 56
German Potato Pancakes, 38
Hollandaise Sauce, 31
Hootenanny Pancake, 50
Italian Sausage Omelet, 20
Louisiana-Style Beignets, 93

Michael's Layered
Mountain Man, 100
Mock Soufflé, 99
My Favorite Pancakes, 49
Old-Fashioned Bread
Pudding, 119
Pennsylvania Dutch
Casserole, 112
Picture Perfect Eggs
and Toast, 25
Quick Breakfast Casserole, 106
Rice Pudding, 116
Sausage Breakfast Bread, 75
Sausage Loaf, 87
Scones, 92
Scotch Eggs, 46
Scrambled Egg Casserole, 108
Spanish Scrambled Eggs, 23
Strawberry and Cream
Crepes, 61
Stuffed Pancakes, 53
Tapas, A Spanish Omelet, 22
Welsh Rarebit, 120
English muffin:
Eggs Benedict, 31
Welsh Rarebit, 120

F
Favorite Mountain Man
Breakfast, 102
Firehouse Hash, 44
Fluffy Apple Pancake, 55
French Toast Dumplings, 58
French Toast Soufflé, 56
filling:
Fruit Filling, 53
Strawberry Filling, 61
Fruit Filling, in Stuffed
Pancakes, 53

G
German Potato Pancakes, 38
gluten free:
Baked Omelet Squares, 97
Basic Omelet, The, 17
Breakfast Hash, 45
Chocolate Crepes, 62
Cornbread Breakfast
Casserole, 103

Cowboy Creamies, 35
Denver Omelet, 19
Dutch Oven Sparkling
     Potatoes, 43
Easy Crust-less Quiche, 30
Favorite Mountain Man
     Breakfast, 102
Firehouse Hash, 44
Italian Sausage Omelet, 20
Michael's Layered
     Mountain Man, 100
Pennsylvania Dutch
     Casserole, 112
Potato Spears, 40
Rice Pudding, 116
Sausage Potato Casserole, 111
Scrambled Egg Casserole, 108
Spanish Scrambled Eggs, 23
Strawberry and Cream
     Crepes, 61
Sunrise Potatoes, 39
Tapas, A Spanish Omelet, 22
Gravy, Country, 71
Gravy, Sausage, 71

H

ham:
     Baked Omelet Squares, 97
     Denver Omelet, 19
     Mock Soufflé, 99
     Scrambled Egg Casserole, 108
Hash, Breakfast, 45
Hash, Firehouse, 44
hazelnut:
     chocolate-hazelnut spread,
          in Stuffed Pancakes, 53
     Cinnamon Hazelnut Braid, 80
Hollandaise Sauce, 31
Homemade Syrup, 50
honey, in Potato Spears, 40
Hootenanny Pancake, 50

I

Italian Sausage Omelet, 20

J

jalapeño pepper, in
     Firehouse Hash, 44

L

Lighting coals, 12
Loaf, Sausage, 87
Louisiana-Style Beignets, 93

M

mayonnaise, in Sausage
     Potato Casserole, 111
Michael's Layered
     Mountain Man, 100
milk, half-and-half, and
          heavy cream:
     Aebleskivers, 59
     Baked Omelet Squares, 97
     Baking Powder Biscuits
          and Gravy, 70
     Banana Nut Bread, 66
     Bread Pudding, 115
     Breakfast Hash, 45
     Brioches du Citron, 76
     Brunch Egg Casserole, 107
     Chocolate Crepes, 62
     Cinnamon Hazelnut Braid, 80
     Classic Quiche Lorraine, 26
     Cornbread Breakfast
          Casserole, 103
     Country Gravy, 71
     Cowboy Creamies, 35
     Doughnuts, 79
     Fluffy Apple Pancake, 55
     French Toast Soufflé, 56
     Hootenanny Pancake, 50
     Louisiana-Style Beignets, 93
     Mock Soufflé, 99
     My Favorite Pancakes, 49
     Old-Fashioned Bread
          Pudding, 119
     Quick Breakfast Casserole, 106
     Rice Pudding, 116
     Sausage Gravy, 71
     Scrambled Egg Casserole, 108
     Spanish Scrambled Eggs, 23
     Strawberry and Cream
          Crepes, 61
     Stuffed Pancakes, 53
     Welsh Rarebit, 120
Mock Soufflé, 99
Mountain Man Breakfast,
     Favorite, 102

Mountain Man, Michael's
     Layered, 100
mushroom:
     Baked Omelet Squares, 97
     Classic Quiche Lorraine, 26
My Favorite Pancakes, 49

N

nuts:
     almond, in Brioches
          du Citron, 76
     hazelnut, in Cinnamon
          Hazelnut Braid, 80
     pecan:
          Banana Nut Bread, 66
          Fluffy Apple Pancake, 55
     walnut:
          Aloha Bread, 67
          Banana Bread, 65
          Cranberry Orange
               Nut Bread, 69

O

Old-Fashioned Bread Pudding, 119
olive, in Baked Omelet Squares, 97
Omelet Squares, Baked, 97
onion:
     Baked Omelet Squares, 97
     Blue Cheese Quiche, 28
     Breakfast Burritos, 36
     Breakfast Hash, 45
     Classic Quiche Lorraine, 26
     Cornbread Breakfast
          Casserole, 103
     Cowboy Creamies, 35
     Denver Omelet, 19
     Dutch Oven Sparkling
          Potatoes, 43
     Easy Crust-less Quiche, 30
     Favorite Mountain Man
          Breakfast, 102
     Firehouse Hash, 44
     German Potato Pancakes, 38
     Italian Sausage Omelet, 20
     Michael's Layered
          Mountain Man, 100
     Pennsylvania Dutch
          Casserole, 112
     Rice and Sausage Especial, 113

onion (continued)
   Sausage Loaf, 87
   Sausage Potato Casserole, 111
   Scrambled Egg Casserole, 108
   Sunrise Potatoes, 39
   Tapas, A Spanish Omelet, 22
Orange Nut Bread, Cranberry, 69

P
pancake:
   Fluffy Apple Pancake, 55
   German Potato Pancakes, 38
   Hootenanny Pancake, 50
   My Favorite Pancakes, 49
   Stuffed Pancakes, 53
pancake mix, in Fluffy
   Apple Pancake, 55
Pastry, Danish, 94
pecan:
   Banana Nut Bread, 66
   Fluffy Apple Pancake, 55
Pennsylvania Dutch
   Casserole, 112
Picture Perfect Eggs and Toast, 25
pie crust, in Classic Quiche
   Lorraine, 26
pineapple:
   Aloha Bread, 67
   Old-Fashioned Bread
      Pudding, 119
potato:
   Breakfast Burritos, 36
   Breakfast Hash, 45
   Cowboy Creamies, 35
   Dutch Oven Sparkling
      Potatoes, 43
   Favorite Mountain Man
      Breakfast, 102
   Firehouse Hash, 44
   German Potato Pancakes, 38
   Michael's Layered
      Mountain Man, 100
   Pennsylvania Dutch
      Casserole, 112
   Potato Spears, 40
   Sausage Potato Casserole, 111
   Scotch Eggs, 46
   Sunrise Potatoes, 39
   Tapas, A Spanish Omelet, 22

pudding:
   Apple Pudding, 122
   Bread Pudding, 115
   Old-Fashioned Bread
      Pudding, 119
   Rice Pudding, 116

Q
quiche:
   Blue Cheese Quiche, 28
   Classic Quiche Lorraine, 26
   Easy Crust-less Quiche, 30
Quick Breakfast Casserole, 106

R
raisin:
   Bread Pudding, 115
   Cinnamon Bread, 83
   Rice Pudding, 116
raspberry jelly, in Danish Pastry, 94
rice:
   Rice and Sausage Especial, 113
   Rice Pudding, 116
   Sausage Loaf, 87
Rolls, Cinnamon, 84

S
Sauce, Hollandaise, 31
sausage:
   ground:
      Breakfast Burritos, 36
      Cornbread Breakfast
         Casserole, 103
      Favorite Mountain Man
         Breakfast, 102
      Italian Sausage Omelet, 20
      Michael's Layered
         Mountain Man, 100
      Quick Breakfast
         Casserole, 106
      Rice and Sausage
         Especial, 113
      Sausage Biscuit Bites, 72
      Sausage Breakfast Bread, 75
      Sausage Gravy, 71
      Sausage Loaf, 87
      Scotch Eggs, 46
   smoked, in Sausage Potato
      Casserole, 111

scallion, in Spanish
   Scrambled Eggs, 23
Scones, 92
Scotch Eggs, 46
Seasoning your Dutch oven, 12
Soufflé, French Toast, 56
Soufflé, Mock, 99
sour cream:
   Blue Cheese Quiche, 28
   Breakfast Hash, 45
   Firehouse Hash, 44
   Sausage Potato Casserole, 111
Spanish Omelet, Tapas, A, 22
Spanish Scrambled Eggs, 23
Sparkling Potatoes,
   Dutch Oven, 43
Sprite, in Dutch Oven
   Sparkling Potatoes, 43
Storing your Dutch oven, 12
strawberry:
   Strawberry and Cream
      Crepes, 61
   Strawberry Filling, 61
Stuffed Pancakes, 53
Sunrise Potatoes, 39
Syrup, Homemade, 50

T
Tapas, A Spanish Omelet, 22
tomato, in Spanish
   Scrambled Eggs, 23
tortilla, in Breakfast Burritos, 36

U
Useful tools, 11

W
walnut:
   Aloha Bread, 67
   Banana Bread, 65
   Cranberry Orange
      Nut Bread, 69
Welsh Rarebit, 120
whipped cream:
   Fruit Filling, 53
   Old-Fashioned Bread
      Pudding, 119
   Strawberry Filling, 61